WARRIORS
Through the Ages

Bruce LaFontaine

Dover Publications, Inc.
Mineola, New York

About the Author

Bruce LaFontaine is the writer and illustrator of thirty-five nonfiction children's books. He specializes in the subject areas of history, science, transportation, and architecture for middle readers, ages eight through twelve. Mr. LaFontaine's published works include *Modern Experimental Aircraft*, *Famous Buildings of Frank Lloyd Wright*, *Great Inventors and Inventions*, and many others. His book, *Exploring the Solar System,* published in 1999, was selected by *Astronomy* magazine as one of the twenty-one best astronomy books for children. In the same year, Mr. LaFontaine was profiled in *Something About the Author*, a hardcover publication featuring prominent authors and illustrators in the field of children's literature. Mr. LaFontaine served as a staff sergeant in the United States Air Force during the Vietnam era. He has worked in the Rochester, New York area as a writer, illustrator, and art director for twenty-five years.

Published in Canada by General Publishing Company, Ltd., 895 Don Mills Road, 400-2 Park Centre, Toronto, Ontario M3C 1W3.
Published in the United Kingdom by David & Charles, Brunel House, Forde Close, Newton Abbot, Devon, TQ12 4PU.

Bibliographical Note

Warriors Through the Ages is a new work, first published by Dover Publications, Inc. in 2002.

DOVER *Pictorial Archive* SERIES

International Standard Book Number: 0-486-42071-X

Manufactured in the United States of America
Dover Publications, Inc., 31 East 2nd Street, Mineola, N.Y. 11501

INTRODUCTION

Warfare has shaped the civilizations of both the ancient and modern world, with the clash between different cultures for territory and resources a constant factor in human development. Technological advances can also be tied to the conflicts between nations since they have often been driven by the imperatives of war. This book chronicles both the cultural and technological history of civilization as represented by the individual battle-seasoned warrior. It covers a period of 3,500 years, from ancient Egypt to World War II.

The soldiers depicted in this book fall into distinct eras and time periods. The ancient world, including the "Classical" periods of Greece and Rome, lasted from approximately 2,000 B.C. to the fall of Rome in A.D. 475. From that date until around A.D. 900, the European world fell into the "Dark Ages," a time of ignorance, superstition, and brutal tribal warfare. During "Medieval" times (A.D. 1000 to A.D. 1475), the clans and tribes of Europe were shaping themselves through constant warfare into the nations of the modern world. A new age, the "Renaissance," began around A.D. 1500 and led to the "Age of Enlightenment" of the seventeenth and eighteenth centuries. Both periods were marked by constant warfare. Armed conflict continued throughout Europe and other parts of the world well into the modern era of the nineteenth and twentieth centuries.

Ancient warriors fought with primitive weapons of wood, bronze, and iron. The spear, shield, bow, sword, and axe were used to engage the enemy in close combat. Soldiers wore body armor to shield themselves from the cuts and blows of these weapons. These protective coverings evolved from thickly padded cloth and leather to "scale armor" (made by attaching metal plates to a leather coat) and iron "chain mail" (ringlets of metal attached together to form a loose fitting overshirt). "Plate armor" was worn by medieval knights and often encased the entire body in a metal suit. Gunpowder and firearms were introduced by the Chinese around A.D. 1200 and in Europe around A.D. 1300, changing the face of warfare forever. The age of the armored warrior was ended by the sheer power and ability of cannon artillery and handheld muskets to inflict serious damage.

The warfare methods of the modern era have become more fully mechanized and brutally efficient at the mass destruction of opposing armies and national resources. Where conflicts of the past were measured in thousands of battle casualties (killed and wounded), they are now measured in *hundreds of thousands* or even *millions*. The last great war, World War II (1939–1945), was fought with such fearsome new weapons as armored battle tanks, long-range artillery, rockets, submarines, and massed formations of bomber aircraft. The two aggressor nations of that conflict, Germany and Japan, paid a terrible price for their efforts at conquest. By 1945, the great cities of Germany lay in ruins from continuous aerial bombardment by warplanes of the Allied nations. Japan was left in ashes from American bomber fleets dropping incendiary (fire) bombs and a new super-weapon—the atomic bomb.

Despite advances in the technology of war, the actual waging of war has always depended on the skill and courage of the warrior—the individual soldier who must face an enemy in armed combat. Over the ages, warriors have fought for their tribes and clans, pharaohs, kings and emperors, nations, religions, and ideologies. They have been the instruments of the political and military powers that helped create our modern world.

HITTITE WARRIOR VS. EGYPTIAN WARRIOR (FACING PAGE), BATTLE OF KADESH, 1286 B.C.

Hittite Warrior

The Hittite people established an empire in the middle-eastern region of Anatolia, now part of the modern-day nation of Turkey. This civilization reached its peak between 1600 B.C. and 1300 B.C. The Hittites are generally believed to have initiated the widespread use of iron weapons and tools. Prior to the introduction of iron, the metal alloy "bronze" was used by ancient civilizations. Bronze is a mixture of copper and tin, metals that are plentiful and easily smelted—i.e., extracted and refined by heat from the natural rock ore in which they are found. Bronze is a much softer metal than iron, and will bend or break under conditions in which iron will remain intact and durable.

The iron weapons of the Hittites gave them a distinct advantage in battle over their adversaries who still used bronze swords, shields, and armor. An iron-tipped arrow used by the Hittite archer shown above could easily penetrate the bronze armor of an enemy soldier. The bows of this era were generally made from a composite of wood, horn, and dried animal tendons held together with a primitive glue. They could shoot an arrow out to an accurate range of about 250 yards. Despite their iron weaponry, the Hittite army was defeated at the Battle of Kadesh c. 1286 B.C. by the Egyptian army under the command of Pharaoh Rameses II.

Egyptian Warrior

The great civilization of Egypt reigned supreme as a political and military power in the Middle East and Africa for over 2,000 years. Unified under its first Pharaoh Menes (also known as Narmer) in 2900 B.C., it remained a powerful nation until 330 B.C. when it was conquered by the Persian Empire. Egypt was ruled by a long line of pharaohs, considered god-kings, through a series of hereditary dynasties. The zenith of Egyptian power was reached under Pharaoh Rameses II, who reigned for over fifty years.

The Egyptian foot soldier shown above is armed with a bronze-tipped spear and a short double-edged bronze sword. Shields could be made of solid wood or stiffened cowhide stretched over a wooden frame. Many Egyptian soldiers went into battle with no body armor, clothed only in a loincloth wrapped around the waist. For additional protection, some warriors also wore a thick leather vest around the torso, and a leather or bronze helmet.

SPARTAN WARRIOR VS. PERSIAN WARRIOR (FACING PAGE), BATTLE OF THERMOPYLAE, 480 B.C.

Spartan Warrior

The ancient civilization of Greece was made up of a number of city-states. Chief among these independent kingdoms were the cities of Athens and Sparta. Although they were often at war with each other as was demonstrated by the two Peloponnesian Wars (460–445 B.C. and 432–404 B.C.), they united to fight the Persians—their common foe—led by King Xerxes who invaded Greece in 480 B.C. with an army of 180,000 troops. In their march toward Athens, the Persians were met by a force of 7,000 Greek "hoplites," heavily armed infantry soldiers, guarding the mountain pass at Thermopylae. In a rear guard action, a band of 300 Spartans under their king Leonidas delayed the Persian advance by fighting to the death against the overwhelming numbers of the invaders. Although the Persians took Athens, they were defeated by the Greeks at the naval battle of Salamis later that year.

The social structure of Sparta was rigid, harsh, and militaristic. It was divided into two classes: the slaves were called "helots," and free citizens were known as "Spartiates." All male Spartiates were compelled to undergo rigorous military training and serve in the Spartan army as citizen-soldiers. The Spartan soldier depicted above carries a double-edged steel curved sword about twenty inches long and a steel-tipped spear. He wears a Thracian*-style helmet that protects most of his head and face, and a breastplate or "cuirass" covering his back and chest, both made of bronze. His legs are protected by "greaves," also made from bronze. He carries into battle a large round shield of bronze-covered wood.

*In ancient times, the Thracians were a community of tribes located in what is now Bulgaria and Turkey.

Persian "Immortal" Imperial Guard

The Persian empire encompassed a vast territory covering most of the Middle East, as well as parts of Africa, India, and Europe. It was founded by the emperor Cyrus the Great in 539 B.C. after his conquest of Babylon. In 490 B.C., the Persians led by King Darius I invaded the Greek mainland intent on conquering both Athens and Sparta. They were defeated at the Battle of Marathon by the Athenian army.

The Persians again invaded Greece in 480 B.C., this time under Xerxes, the successor to Darius I. The army marched on to Athens, burning the city and occupying the territory. However, their fleet of warships and supply vessels was destroyed later that year by the Greek navy at the Battle of Salamis. For lack of a steady supply line, the Persian army was forced to withdraw from Greece. Finally, in 331 B.C. the Persian empire was conquered and absorbed by the armies of the Macedonian military genius, Alexander the Great.

The Persian warrior depicted above is a member of the "Immortals," an elite corps of 10,000 highly trained imperial soldiers. He is armed with a steel sword and steel-tipped spear. He wears a bronze helmet and carries a bronze shield. His body is protected by a long shirt or "tunic" made of thick leather studded with iron rivets.

LEGIONARY SOLDIER VS. WARRIOR OF HANNIBAL'S CARTHAGE (FACING PAGE), BATTLE OF CANNAE, 216 B.C.

Legionary Soldier of the Roman Republic

The Roman republic rose to power during the years after the death of Alexander the Great in 323 B.C. By 280 B.C., Rome ruled most of the Mediterranean region, its power established by a large and disciplined army, organized into "legions" of 5,000 soldiers. A legionary soldier was a full-time professional who typically served for twenty-five years. The greatest challenge to the authority of pre-imperial Rome came from the North African city-state known as Carthage. Located in modern-day Tunisia, Carthage was a wealthy maritime empire. The "Punic Wars"—a series of military conflicts between Rome and Carthage—occurred during the period from 264 to 146 B.C. The First Punic War began with the successful Roman invasion of the Carthaginian-held island of Sicily in 264 B.C. The Second

Punic War was led by the great Carthaginian general Hannibal Barca beginning in 218 B.C. The Third Punic War (149–146 B.C.) ended in the complete destruction of Carthage by Roman legions under the command of General Scipio Africanus.

The legionary pictured above wears a tunic made from "chain mail," small iron links riveted together to form a barrier against sword cuts. His bronze helmet is designed to protect the head, face, and back of the neck. His oval shield, called a "scutum," is constructed of wood and bronze, and is large enough to protect most of his body against oncoming arrows, spears, and stones. His weapons are a short double-edged sword called a "gladius" and a throwing spear called a "hasta."

Warrior from Hannibal's Carthage

The city of Carthage was founded in 814 B.C. on the North African coast. It was the center of a powerful maritime trading empire that extended throughout the Mediterranean area. A clash with the expanding Roman republic was inevitable. In the First Punic War with Rome, Carthage was defeated and lost control of their island territory of Sicily. The Second Punic War began in 218 B.C., under the leadership of the brilliant military tactician Hannibal Barca. Leading his army across Spain and Gaul (France), he invaded Italy by crossing the Alps. Among his forces were squadrons of armored elephants, an adversary never seen before by the Roman legions. Hannibal defeated a large Roman army at the decisive Battle of Cannae in 216 B.C.,

but did not capture Rome itself. He held most of Italy for ten years, but was recalled to Carthage to defend against a Roman counterattack. His forces were defeated at the Battle of Zama in 202 B.C.

Shown above on their trek through the Alps is a Carthaginian archer and an armored war elephant. The bowman is protected by a tunic of "scale armor," a leather garment with overlapping bronze plates riveted in place. The elephant is wearing a thick leather blanket with iron and bronze armor attached at various points. His skull is covered by an iron-spiked shield. A charging elephant protected by armor could easily break up the battle formations of the Roman legions.

LEGIONARY OF IMPERIAL ROME VS. CELTIC WARRIOR OF BRITANNIA (FACING PAGE), A.D. 60

Roman Imperial Legionary

Rome attained the pinnacle of its power and influence during its Imperial era, when a series of emperors extended its hold into most of the known world, transforming it from a republic into an empire. In A.D. 43, under the emperor Claudius, Rome invaded the island of Britannia, which was occupied by a number of fierce Celtic tribes who inhabited northern and western Europe. By A.D. 61, after numerous battles and revolts by the native Celts, southern Britain came firmly under the control of the Roman legions based there. However, they were never able to subdue the Scottish highland tribes—the Picts—of the north. To prevent raids by these "barbarians," the emperor Hadrian ordered construction of a stone wall that stretched from Britain's west to its east coast, dividing the unpacified north from the south. "Hadrian's Wall," as it is known, was built

between A.D. 122 and 128, and was fifteen feet high, ten feet wide and seventy-five miles long. It was fortified with stone block-houses at regular intervals garrisoned by legionary troops. Portions of this famous barrier still exist in modern Britain.

The Imperial legionary shown above wears the standard body armor of the era, the breastplate known as a "Lorica Segmenta," consisting of a series of wraparound steel bands held together with rivets and leather straps. This jointed armor allowed for considerable freedom of movement as well as protection. The soldier also wears a Gallic-style steel helmet with wide cheek flaps. His large rectangular, curved shield, or scutum, was made of wood, metal, and leather. He is armed with a throwing javelin called a "pilum," the "gladius" short sword, and a dagger or "pugio."

Celtic Warrior of Britannia

The Celts inhabited many parts of Europe from as far north as Denmark to as far south as Spain. Their principal strongholds, however, were in Britain and Ireland. They were accomplished artisans in metalworking and textiles. Although fearless in battle, they were never able to unite into a single cohesive fighting force because of their independent and clannish natures. These fierce and skilled warriors fought as much among themselves as they did against the invading Roman legions. Finally, a successful revolt by the Iceni—a Celtic tribe—occurred in A.D. 61, led by their legendary warrior queen Boudica. Although her forces defeated the Ninth Legion and destroyed Roman-held London, they were eventually overcome by the more disciplined fighting tactics of the Romans.

The Celtic warrior pictured carries a leaf-shaped steel sword around thirty inches long, and a metal-reinforced wooden shield. He wears no body armor other than the stylized, horned bronze helmet. In fact, many Celtic warriors chose to go into battle completely naked as a sign of their bravery and fighting prowess.

LEGIONARY CENTURION VS. HORSEMAN OF ATTILLA THE HUN (FACING PAGE), A.D. 453

Legionary Centurion of the Holy Roman Empire

In A.D. 324, the emperor Constantine, the first Christian emperor of Rome and founder of Constantinople, declared Christianity the official state religion. Prior to this edict, the empire had already been divided into eastern and western spheres by the emperor Diocletian (A.D. 286), who perceived that his dominion was so vast as to be too vulnerable to be safely ruled by a single head. As sole Emperor of the West some forty years later, Constantine's support of the Catholic Church enabled it to become a powerful entity within this new Roman world. And the head of the Church—the pope—was second only to the emperor in political power.

The rigid structure and disciplined tactics of the Roman legion continued into the Christian era. The heart of the legion was the "centurion," very much like a modern-day sergeant, who commanded a group of eighty men known as a "century." A "cohort" was a larger battle unit consisting of six centuries. Ten cohorts made up a "legion" of between 5,500 and 6,000 legionary or foot soldiers. Unlike the legionaries, the centurions did not march but rode on horseback. The centurion depicted above wears a steel breast and back-plate, a plumed late Imperial-style helmet, and steel greaves to protect his legs. He is armed with a "gladius" (sword) and a "pugio" (dagger).

Horseman of Attilla the Hun

In the era of Christian Rome, the Holy Roman Empire was attacked by a number of barbarian armies including those of the Ostrogoths, Visigoths, and Vandals. However, the greatest threat to Rome came from the East in the form of the horse-mounted army of Attilla the Hun, known as the "Scourge of God" by his adversaries. The Huns (or *Hsiung-nu*) were a confederation of nomadic tribes that dominated central Asia for two centuries about 2,300 years ago. They were brutal and merciless in warfare, routinely killing men, women, and children in the conquered territories. Attilla's army moved swiftly with a large contingent of mounted cavalry. The horseman shown above carries a steel broadsword, and is armored with a metal-studded breastplate and iron helmet. Mounted archers also comprised a large segment of Attilla's forces.

In A.D. 451, Attilla invaded Gaul (France) but was defeated by a combined army of Roman legions and Visigoths under their king Theodoric. One year later, Attilla's Huns swept into Italy intent on destroying Rome itself. Before the actual attack on Rome ensued, however, he was persuaded to withdraw by Pope Leo I. Some historians believe that Attilla was awed by the pope's "holiness," while others are convinced he feared the mystical or supernatural powers of the Church. Still others contend that his army was too weakened by battle losses and deaths by plague to continue.

TEUTONIC MAN-AT-ARMS OF SAXONY VS. FRANKISH WARRIOR OF CHARLEMAGNE (FACING PAGE), A.D. 788

Teutonic Man-at-Arms of Saxony

The end of the great empire of Rome occurred in A.D. 476 with the overthrow of Romulus Augustus, the last Emperor of the West. For the next 500 years, Europe struggled through the "Dark Ages," a period of conflict between warring tribes and cultures attempting to establish their power and territorial borders. The modern nations of Europe had not yet formed, and superstition, ignorance, cruelty, and fear prevailed over the western world during this era.

The Germanic or Teutonic people who had emigrated from Scandinavia (Denmark, Sweden, Norway) were divided into a series of individual kingdoms, among them Saxony, Bavaria, Westphalia, and Frisia. Conflict with the Franks (French), their neighbors to the west, was ongoing. Pictured above is a "man-at-arms," or common soldier, from the kingdom of Saxony. He wears a wide-brimmed iron helmet, a long tunic of iron chain mail, and a shorter "surcoat" (overshirt) of iron-studded leather. His chief weapon is a fearsome war axe, able to cleave through both chain mail and plate armor, and he also carries a long dagger for close combat.

Frankish Warrior of Charles the Great (Charlemagne)

The greatest military power to emerge during the Dark Ages was the kingdom of the Franks (modern-day France). At the Battles of Tours and Poitiers in A.D. 732, Charles Martel, leader of the Franks, defeated an invading Muslim army intent on conquering western Europe. His son, Pepin the Short, was crowned king in 754. In turn, Pepin's son Charles (later to be known as Charles the Great or Charlemagne) became king in 768. He expanded the Frankish territory into other areas of Europe by defeating the Lombards of Italy in 774, the Teutonic (German) states of Bavaria and Saxony in 788, and the Avars of Hungary in 796. In A.D. 800, with the blessing of the Catholic pope, Charlemagne was crowned Emperor of the West of the Holy Roman Empire. Upon his death in 814, the Frankish kingdom began to dissolve into civil war among the various factions vying for power.

The Frankish warrior illustrated stands guard at a wooden hill fort, a series of garrisons established around its territorial borders. He is armed with a sword and a poleaxe. The poleaxe was especially effective against mounted cavalry, its long blade able to reach out and knock a horseman out of the saddle.

IRISH WARRIOR VS. VIKING INVADER (FACING PAGE), BATTLE OF CLONTARF, A.D. 1014

Irish Warrior

The Ireland of the early medieval period (A.D. 900 to 1200) was comprised of independent clans and kingdoms of the indigenous Celtic tribes, who were subject to a steady series of raids and invasions by their neighbors to the north—the infamous Vikings. The Norsemen established towns and colonies throughout Ireland, while remaining constantly at war with the native Irish. In 1002, an Irish chieftain, Brian Boru, united the Irish clans and was crowned *Ard Ri* (the Gaelic term for "High King"). He led his forces in 1014 in a critical battle to crush the Viking confederacy that was then rooted in Ireland. Just outside Dublin near the village of Clontarf,

Brian Boru's Irish warriors finally routed the Norse invaders. Despite their largely adversarial relationship over the 200-year period of Viking settlement in Ireland, the Scandinavian Norse and native Irish intermarried, contributing to the high percentage of fair-skinned blonde or red-haired Irish of today.

The Irish warrior depicted above is sharpening his two-handed battle sword. It was a savage weapon, over fifty inches long and able to cut a wide swathe of destruction among enemy warriors. This soldier also carries a long dagger, or "dirk," and wears a tunic of protective chain-mail armor.

Viking Warrior

The famous Viking warriors were essentially a seafaring race from the Scandinavian countries of Denmark, Sweden, and Norway. In their fast and durable long-ships, they were also intrepid explorers and colonists, reaching the coast of North America over 400 years before Columbus. They established settlements in Britain, Ireland, France, and Spain, and even ventured into the Mediterranean. They also sailed inland up the Rus River as far east as Moscow in Russia. Both dreaded and respected as ruthless warriors, the sight of a Viking long-ship caused panic among the coastal towns of Europe.

The Viking chieftain pictured above is armed with a battle-ax and long sword. His leather tunic is covered with riveted iron plates for protection, and he wears a stylized, winged-steel helmet. The weapons, jewelry, and tools of the Norse culture were finely wrought and decorated with intricate patterns of interlocking loops and complex geometric patterns.

SAXON MAN-AT-ARMS VS. NORMAN KNIGHT (FACING PAGE), BATTLE OF HASTINGS, 1066

Saxon Man-at-Arms of King Harold of Wessex

The Anglo-Saxon people migrated from the European mainland to the island of Britain around A.D. 600, establishing a series of individual kingdoms, and eventually becoming the dominant culture. The Vikings also invaded and colonized parts of Britain, and in 866, a large Viking army invaded and captured the city of York and the surrounding territory. After a series of battles, the Vikings suffered a sound defeat from the Saxon king Alfred the Great, resulting in a partition of Britain into Viking and Saxon territory. By 1066, Saxon king Harold of Wessex had repelled Danish invasions and consolidated Anglo-Saxon power in Britain. Harold's army was weakened by his battles

against the Danes, however, and fell prey to attack by the Norman knights of William, Duke of Normandy. The Normans invaded in 1066 and defeated the Saxons under King Harold at the Battle of Hastings. William was crowned king of England, and Norman nobles assumed the power of the Saxon barons and landowners.

The Saxon man-at-arms shown above carries a double-bladed battle-ax and a broad sword. He is protected by an iron helmet and padded leather tunic. He stands by a defensive "breastworks," a dirt wall embedded with sharpened timber poles designed to break up the charge of mounted knights.

Norman Knight of William, Duke of Normandy

The coastal province of Normandy was one of the independent kingdoms of the medieval era that existed in what is now the nation of France. It was granted to the Vikings in 911 to prevent further incursions into French territory. In 1066 William, Duke of Normandy, invaded Britain with an army of bowmen, spearmen, and horse-mounted knights. At the Battle of Hastings, the Normans defeated the Saxon defenders, enabling Duke William to assume the title of king of England. Norman power and culture gradually prevailed and eclipsed that of the Saxons.

The Norman knight depicted astride his warhorse is protected by a long coat of chain mail. He carries the teardrop-shaped shield that was common during this era, and he is armed with a broadsword and a lance—the principal weapon used with great efficiency during a cavalry charge.

SPANISH CROSSBOWMAN VS. MOORISH WARRIOR (FACING PAGE), BATTLE OF ZALLACA, 1088

Spanish Crossbowman

The Islamic kingdoms of Africa and the Middle East arose after the death of the prophet Muhammad in A.D. 632, when Abu Bakr, the "caliph" or first deputy of the prophet, sought to spread the new faith through a series of military invasions. Eventually, the Muslims conquered the Middle East, Persia, the Arabian peninsula, and northern Africa. In 711, they finally turned their attention on Europe, with Gibraltar being used as a staging area by the Berber general Tarik and his Moorish army to launch the conquest of Spain. (In fact, "Gibraltar" was originally named *Jebel-al-Tarik*, or "Mount of Tarik.") The largest incursion of Islamic power occurred in 732, when an advancing Islamic force reached France, and was met by an army commanded by the Frankish leader Charles Martel. The invaders were roundly defeated at the battles of Tours and Poitiers, thus ending Muslim efforts to conquer western Europe. Nonetheless, the Moors were able to make large territorial gains in Spain, so that by 756 the Umayyad tribes had taken the city of Cordoba and its environs. By A.D. 912, this European kingdom of the Moors had become a powerful and well-established Muslim province. For the next 400 years, Spanish defenders and invading Moors clashed for control of Spain.

Pictured above is a Spanish "crossbowman" atop a castle wall. The crossbow was a powerful weapon with long range, accuracy, and penetrating power. Its only drawback was that it could not be loaded and fired as quickly as a conventional bow.

Moorish Swordsman

By 1046, the Almoravid Berbers had supplanted the Ummayed tribes to become the most powerful Muslim force in Christian Spain. At the Battle of Zallaca in 1088, they defeated the forces of King Alfonso of Aragon under the command of the legendary Spanish knight "El Cid." In 1098, while attempting to take the city of Valencia, the Moors were this time overcome by victorious Spanish forces, led once again by El Cid. After their defeat at the Battle of Alhambra in 1492, the Moors were finally driven out of Spain.

A Moorish warrior is illustrated above holding a two-handed scimitar. A fearsome weapon about fifty-five inches long, it was intended for slashing rather than stabbing. He wears a round steel breastplate to protect his midsection.

MUSLIM WARRIOR VS. CHRISTIAN CRUSADER (FACING PAGE), BATTLE OF ACRE, 1191

Muslim Warrior of the Sultan Saladin

War between the Christian and Islamic nations of medieval times took the form of a series of crusades by Christian knights to free the Holy City of Jerusalem, which had been captured by the Muslim Turks after the fall of Rome. In 1095, after Muslims banned Christian pilgrims from visiting this sacred religious site, Pope Urban II called upon the Christian kingdoms of Europe to free the Holy Land. For the next 200 years, crusaders and Islamic warriors battled for control of this area. In total, three great Crusades and five lesser Crusades took place between 1096 and 1291.

The first of the great Crusades was launched by a combined army of European and Byzantine forces beginning in 1096. After three years of brutal warfare, the crusaders recaptured Jerusalem and set up a series of Christian kingdoms in Palestine. The Second Crusade was initiated by German and French armies in 1147 who attempted to capture the Muslim city of Damascus. They were defeated by the Islamic forces.

Shown above is an Muslim warrior of this era, dressed in a coat of chain mail, a steel breastplate and helmet, and carrying a curved scimitar sword. He is holding a battle lance with the crescent moon-and-star emblem of Islam.

Christian Crusader of King Richard I of England

The third Great Crusade began in 1189, two years after the Muslim recapture of Jerusalem by the armies of Saladin, sultan of Egypt and Syria, who was also a brilliant military tactician. Of all the crusades, it was the most elaborately equipped, with three great armies led by the Roman emperor and German king, Frederick Barbarossa (also the most accomplished soldier of his time), King Phillip II of France, and Richard the Lion-Hearted of England. For such an enormous effort, it ultimately succeeded little in its goals. In 1191, the crusaders captured the vital port city of Acre, near Jerusalem. After a year-long battle for Jerusalem, King Richard and Saladin signed a treaty allowing Christians to visit the Holy City.

The Fourth Crusade began in 1202 with Christian armies marching against Muslim Egypt and Syria. It ended in 1204 with the recapture of Turkish-held Constantinople. In 1212, a disas-

trous "Children's Crusade" resulted in the deaths or slavery of about 30,000 Christian children, not one over twelve years old when they first set out. Four more lesser Crusades occurred between 1221 and 1291, with Jerusalem alternating between Muslim and Christian control.

The crusader depicted wears a complete suit of chain-mail armor and a steel "Great Helm" that covers and protects his face and head. His teardrop-shaped shield is typical of European shields of the era. His principal weapon is the broadsword, made of steel and about thirty-six inches long. The guard between the blade and the hilt is cross-shaped, or "cruci-form," honoring the symbol of Christianity. To ward off the intense heat of the desert sun, the crusader and his warhorse both wear cloth surcoats, also emblazoned with the Christian cross.

MONGOL INVADER VS. CHINESE DEFENDER (FACING PAGE), 1215

Mongol Invader on Horseback

While the West was embroiled in numerous wars during the medieval period, the eastern civilizations were also battling to establish territorial kingdoms. The ancient civilization of China was engaged in a constant series of border wars with invading barbarian tribes. The most powerful of these tribes were the Mongols of central Asia, nomads who wandered the open plains and deserts of the region, and were superb horseman and fearless warriors. In 1206, the tribes were united under the leadership of the warrior Tamujin who took the name "Ghengis Khan," meaning Great Ruler. The army of the Khan invaded China in 1211, capturing the capital city of Beijing in 1215. By 1217, most of China and Korea was under Mongol control. Upon the death of Ghengis Khan in 1227, his empire was extended into Europe and the Middle East by his sons Batu and Ogadai, and his grandson Kublai. Their army, known as the "Golden Horde," conquered territory as far west as Poland, Russia, and Hungary, and as far south as Turkey, Persia, and Syria.

Chinese Defender on the Great Wall

To guard against invasion by the barbarian tribes from the grassy treeless plains—or steppes—to the west, China constructed a massive stone barrier along its border. Finished in 214 B.C., the "Great Wall" extended 1,600 miles over the mountains and valleys of western China, averaging thirty feet high and twenty feet wide. At regular intervals along the wall, forty-foot watchtowers were built and manned by soldiers. Its original purpose was to guard against the *Hsiung-nu* tribes, known as the Huns to Europeans. Despite the Great Wall's for-

midable appearance, the invading armies of Ghengis Khan penetrated the wall through one of its gates. The Mongol control of China ended in 1386 with a successful revolt by the Chinese, and the establishment of the famous Ming Dynasty.

The Chinese defender atop the Great Wall wears a wide-brimmed iron helmet and armor made of metal plates riveted to a padded cloth tunic. He is armed with a sword and a fighting-knife mounted on a wooden staff.

ENGLISH LONGBOWMAN VS. FRENCH KNIGHT (FACING PAGE), HUNDRED YEARS' WAR, BATTLE OF CRÉCY, 1346

English Longbowman of King Edward III

A series of military conflicts between England and France began about 1337 and continued until 1453. They were collectively known as the "Hundred Years' War," and were instigated by Edward III, King of England, who believed he had a claim to the French throne through the right of hereditary succession. The first significant clash was marked by an English naval victory at the Battle of Sluys in 1340. Edward's army invaded France in 1346 and met the French forces at the Battle of Crécy. The English troops were fewer in number than the French, comprised mainly of men-at-arms and archers, while their adversaries consisted of a sizeable force of mounted knights. Nevertheless, the long-

bows of the English archers proved decisive in a victory over the French.

The English archer illustrated uses a longbow, made from a single piece of yew wood about six feet in length. It had great range and accuracy, and could traverse several hundred yards with steel-tipped arrows capable of piercing the plate armor of French knights. A capable archer could fire ten arrows per minute. With the 5,000 English bowmen at the Battle of Crécy, the air was blackened by the shafts of over 50,000 arrows within the first minute of battle. Thus were the mounted French knights decimated by the concentrated firepower of the English longbow.

French Knight of King Charles V

Archers were again crucial to the English victory in 1356 at the Battle of Poitiers led by King Edward's son, known as the "Black Prince" because he reputedly wore black armor. Considered an embodiment of the chivalric ideal, he was one of the outstanding commanders of the Hundred Years' War. After the death of both Edward and the Black Prince (also named Edward), the French pillaged and raided the English coast, avoiding a more formal and costly battle with England. In 1415 under King Henry V, the English army once more crossed the channel into France. At the Battle of Agincourt, the English were outnumbered three-to-one by the French forces of King Charles VI. Nevertheless, Henry maneuvered the French knights into a closely packed group and broke their charge with a deadly shower of English arrows. His brilliant battle tactics are still taught today at mod-

ern military academies. France was a battleground for the Hundred Years' War with alternating victories for both sides until 1453, when the final French victory at the Battle of Castillon ended the long conflict.

The French knight pictured above wears a tunic and hood of chain mail covered with steel "plate armor," bolted and strapped into position. A "breastplate" protects his chest and back, "pauldrons" cover his shoulders. On his upper arms are "rerebraces," at the elbows are "couters," and on the forearms are "vambraces." His thighs are protected by "cuisses," his knees by "poleyns," the lower legs by "schynbalds," and feet by "sabatons." He is armed with a broadsword and iron "mace," a weapon capable of crushing plate armor and breaking the bones of an adversary.

SPANISH CONQUISTADOR VS. INCA WARRIOR (FACING PAGE), 1530

Spanish Conquistador

While European, Asian, and African kingdoms were rising and falling, great civilizations also were evolving in the Americas. In Mexico and Central America, the Mayan, Olmec, Toltec, and Aztec kingdoms flourished from 2500 B.C. until A.D. 1519. In Peru, the Incas built a mighty empire. But the age of discovery and exploration of the Americas begun by Christopher Columbus in 1492 signaled the end of these native American societies; they could not withstand the aggression of the more technically advanced European explorers and colonists, and were rapidly conquered and absorbed by the invaders.

Spain became a wealthy and powerful seafaring nation from their resource-rich territories in the new world. Great convoys of ships traveled the Atlantic route bringing gold, silver, precious gems, and other valuable resources back to Spain. Instrumental in subduing and pacifying the native American civilizations were the Spanish "conquistadors" (conquerors). Spaniard Hernando Cortez led his force of just 550 conquistadors against the emperor Montezuma and thousands of Aztec warriors in 1519. The Spanish had the advantage of firearms and horse-mounted soldiers, both unknown to the Aztecs. In fact, at their first glimpse of a man on horseback, the Aztecs were confounded, believing they were seeing a single creature—half-man, half-animal.

Inca Warrior of Emperor Atahualpa

The mighty Inca civilization was centered on the high plains of the Andes mountains in Peru, with their territory encompassing parts of the modern nations of Chile, Bolivia, and Ecuador. Cuzco, the capital city of the Incas, contained palaces, temples, roads, and the huge stone fortress of Sacsahuaman. The Inca warrior shown above stands in front of one the thirty-foot walls of the fortress. Constructed from giant blocks of stone, the stones were cut and fitted so precisely that no mortar was needed to join them together. Despite their lack of a written language and wheeled vehicles, these ancient American civilizations managed to build roads, waterways, temples, and huge pyramids rivaling those of ancient Egypt.

The Incas and other Mesoamerican* civilizations also did not have the use of tools and weapons made of strong, durable metals like iron and bronze. They only knew how to smelt gold and silver, softer metals used exclusively for making jewelry and decorative items. The Inca warrior depicted is armed with a wooden club embedded with bits of obsidian, a glass-like mineral that could be chipped to make it razor-sharp. His only protection is provided by a shield, breastplate, and helmet made from stiffened cloth or leather. The Inca empire was conquered in 1532 by a force of 167 Spanish conquistadors under the command of Francisco Pizarro.

*The parts of southern North America occupied by advanced peoples in the time preceding the arrival of Columbus in America.

DUTCH GRENADIER VS. SPANISH MUSKETEER (FACING PAGE), THIRTY YEARS' WAR, 1621

Dutch Grenadier

Following the medieval era, warfare in the Renaissance period (beginning in 1475) took an even more dangerous turn with the introduction of gunpowder and firearms. Although primitive cannon artillery had been invented and used in China as far back as A.D. 1100, and in Europe from around 1340, the use of weapons utilizing gunpowder did not become significant until approximately 1500. The first guns carried by individual soldiers were "matchlock" muskets and pistols, while "flintlock" muskets and pistols that had greater range, accuracy, and firepower were developed soon after.

The matchlock used a lighted fuse, or match—usually made of a piece of rope—to ignite a small amount of powder in an external

priming pan. This, in turn, ignited the gunpowder charge in the barrel to propel the bullet, usually consisting of a lead ball. The flintlock used a piece of flint—a hard rock mineral—striking a metal arm to cause a spark, which ignited the gunpowder in the barrel. The flintlock design made for a more reliable and efficient method of firing a gun, and was used until about 1865.

The Dutch grenadier pictured above fought in the Thirty Years' War (1618–1648). His grenade launcher was a flintlock-operated weapon. Grenades of this era were simple iron bombs filled with gunpowder, fitted with a short fuse. They were either thrown at the enemy or shot from a weapon such as the launcher depicted.

Spanish Musketeer

Most of Europe was embroiled in a major conflict during the seventeenth century known as the "Thirty Years War." It began in 1618, and was primarily a religious struggle between Protestant and Catholic nations. The Protestant cause was represented by the northern provinces of Germany, Bohemia (part of the modern Czech Republic), Sweden, Holland (The Netherlands), Denmark, and England. The Catholic nations were led by the Austro-Hungarian Holy Roman Empire and Spain. By 1635, France had joined in on the side of the Protestants. Although a Catholic nation, France feared the growing power of the Habsburg emperors of Austria-Hungary. The Protestant nations allied with France even-

tually defeated the Catholic powers. The war ended with the Treaty of Westphalia in 1648, which granted the Protestant nations independence and religious freedom.

Shown above is a Spanish musketeer from the era of the Thirty Years' War. He is armed with a matchlock musket and "rapier." A rapier is a thin, straight sword with a flexible double-edged blade. It superseded the larger broadsword of the medieval period because its lighter blade allowed for quicker and more deft handling by the swordsman. The skill of sword-fighting known as "fencing" was based on the use of the rapier. The musketeer also wears a crested Spanish-style steel helmet called a "morion," typical of this period.

ROYALIST CAVALIER VS. ROUNDHEAD SOLDIER (FACING PAGE), ENGLISH CIVIL WAR, BATTLE OF NASEBY, 1645

Royalist Cavalier of King Charles I

The English Civil War (also known as the Puritan Revolution) began in 1642 under the reign of King Charles I. The king and his followers, called "Royalists," believed in the absolute power of the monarchy, while members of the elected body of the English government—the "Parliamentarians"—claimed that they had the authority to make laws governing the land. After a series of clashes between the two, the king dissolved Parliament and arrested leaders of the House of Commons, inciting civil war between the two factions. The first battle

occurred at Edgehill, Warwicshire in 1642, but there was no clear victor in this first encounter.

A Royalist soldier, such as the one above, was called a "cavalier." His arms include a rapier and a flintlock pistol. He also wears an iron breastplate for protection. With the introduction and widespread use of firearms, the steel plate armor of the medieval era became obsolete. With no other armor to weigh them down, soldiers could wear breastplates of thicker iron, often able to stop a musket ball.

Roundhead Soldier of Oliver Cromwell's Army of Parliament

The Parliamentary army was led by a brilliant military general, Oliver Cromwell, whose troops were known as the "New Model Army." His soldiers were called "Roundheads," a name derived from their close-cropped haircuts (reflecting the the Puritans' disapproval of long hair). In 1645, Cromwell led his forces to a resounding victory at the Battle of Naseby. King Charles was arrested but escaped to Scotland where he raised an army to launch a second offensive. This attempt failed and the king was tried for treason and executed in 1649. Oliver Cromwell was appointed Lord Protector of England, and with Parliament, ruled England until 1658. During this period England was a republic, the only time in its 1,000-year history when a member of royalty did not reign as head of state. In 1660, however, the English demanded the restoration of the monarchy. Returning from exile in France, Charles II, the son of the late king, assumed the throne of England.

The Roundhead soldier pictured carries a flintlock weapon as well as a rapier sword. He wears a thick iron breastplate and an iron "Lobster Tail" helmet, so named because of the segmented rear neck guard that resembles a lobster's tail. His face is protected from sword slashes by three vertical iron bars attached to the brim of the helmet.

POLISH KNIGHT VS. RUSSIAN COSSACK WARRIOR (FACING PAGE), 1654

Polish Knight

During the seventeenth century, European nations were still battling for power and land. The Mongols—or Tatars—of central Asia controlled most of Russia until 1480, when Ivan the Great refused to pay tribute to the Tatars and their army withdrew without a battle. But it wasn't until the seventeenth century that Russia changed from a feudal society into a modern western nation. The tsars of the Romanov family had assumed imperial control of the vast Russian territory and were actively trying to expand it even further.

In 1654, an inconclusive border war broke out between Russia and neighboring Poland. Shown above is a mounted Polish knight of this conflict. He is armed with a curved cavalry saber, a very efficient weapon for slashing infantry from horseback. He also carries a flintlock pistol in a saddle-mounted holster. His body armor includes a thick iron breastplate as well as plate armor to protect his thighs and knees. His stylized, winged steel helmet is of the "zischagge" type, popular in such Eastern European countries as Poland, Hungary, Germany, and Russia.

Russian Cossack Warrior

The Cossacks were a fierce tribe of horseback warriors from the steppes of southern Russia. There they formed autonomous communities organized on principles of political freedom and social equality, and gained special privileges as the border guards for the tsars. For the four centuries preceding the Russian Revolution of 1917, free Cossack warriors also helped extend Russia's southern and eastern frontiers. By the late eighteenth century, however, they had lost much of their autonomy and became assimilated as the privileged military class of Russia.

The Cossack warrior depicted above wears a traditional lambskin cap and vest, and carries a saber and flintlock pistol. Cossacks fought in their own Russian military units, and this tradition carried over into World War I where Cossack regiments did battle on the western front against Germany and Austro-Hungary, and in the south against the Ottoman Empire (now Turkey).

AMERICAN SOLDIER VS. BRITISH REDCOAT, REVOLUTIONARY WAR, BATTLE OF SARATOGA, 1777

American Soldier of the Continental Army

In 1775, a rebellion broke out among the British colonists in America who believed they were being unfairly taxed by Great Britain, then under the reign of King George III. British troops were sent to the colonies to quell the unrest, and the first battle between the colonists and the British "redcoats" took place at Lexington, Massachusetts. The American civilian militia was defeated by the highly trained British troops. The acting government for the colonies—the Continental Congress—authorized the formation of a regular army under the command of General George Washington. Soon after, another battle, this time at Bunker Hill near Boston, also resulted in a British victory. Nevertheless, in 1776 the Continental Congress drew up the "Declaration of Independence," asserting that the colonies had become a sovereign nation, free of Great Britain. One of the first American

victories was in 1777, at the Battle of Saratoga in upstate New York. The war continued until the surrender of the British army to General Washington at Yorktown, Virginia in 1781.

The American forces were made up of both regular soldiers of the Continental Army and civilian militia—known as "minutemen"—a reference to their readiness to fight at a minute's notice. The soldier depicted wears the uniform of the Continental Army. His long coat is dark blue with tan trim, and his pants and knee-high leggings are also tan. He carries a flintlock musket fitted with an eighteen-inch long socket musket fitted over the barrel. The musket was loaded by tearing open a gunpowder-filled paper cartridge and pouring the contents into the barrel. A musket ball was dropped into the barrel and firmly tamped into position with a "ramrod" that slides out from under the barrel.

British "Redcoat" of King George III

The British army of this period was a large, well-trained, and disciplined fighting force. They marched into battle in tight ranks and formations, and fired their muskets in simultaneous volleys. This created a wall of lead musket balls able to cripple the lines of enemy soldiers. Volley fire was employed to counter the inherent inaccuracy of the musket with its smooth-bore, non-rifled barrel. Rifled barrels had much greater accuracy and range than smooth-bore weapons, and wouldn't be introduced until the next century.

The military tactics of the American troops were very different from the British. While the British marched into battle in rigid formations, the Americans fought from the cover of rocks, trees, stone walls and fences, fallen logs, and other protective barriers. This allowed them to pick off dozens of enemy soldiers, effectively breaking the advance of their enemy's battle lines. The British commanders were confused and frustrated by the success of the American strategy.

The British soldier shown above is dressed in a bright red coat with white trim. This prompted the nickname "redcoats" for English troops. His pants and stockings are white with black leggings, and he wears a "Tarleton"-style lacquered leather helmet.

FRENCH ARTILLERY OFFICER VS. BRITISH INFANTRYMAN (FACING PAGE), BATTLE OF WATERLOO, 1815

French Artillery Officer of Napoleon's Grande Armée

At the beginning of the nineteenth century, France and Great Britain were the two most powerful nations in Europe. War between them was an inevitable outcome of their aggressive empire-building. Out of the French Revolution of 1789, a brilliant military commander, Napoleon Bonaparte, rose through the ranks of the French army. Napoleon eventually became emperor of France and master of most of continental Europe. His Grande Armée not only defeated the armies of Europe, but extended French military power into Russia and Africa.

In 1797, Napoleon's armies defeated the Austrians to capture Italy. The following year, he invaded and conquered Egypt in an attempt to disrupt British trade and supply routes to their vast empire in India. In 1799, the nations of Britain, Russia, Austria,

and Turkey formed an alliance to stop Napoleon's aggression. Two decisive battles were fought in 1805, one on land and one at sea. Napoleon's greatest land battle was his victory over the Austrians and Russians at the Battle of Austerlitz. At sea, the British navy under the brilliant Admiral Lord Nelson defeated the French fleet at the Battle of Trafalgar.

The French officer illustrated wears a finely tailored, colorful as well as decorative uniform. His "epaulets" (shoulder boards) have silk tassels. Hanging from his silk sash is a "sabertache," a decorative bag for holding messages and personal items. The most elaborate items of Napoleonic era uniforms were the headgear: the "shako" worn by the officer is festooned with badges, chains, plumes, and ruffled silk.

British Infantryman of Lord Wellington

From 1805 to 1811, Napoleon's army continued to win land battles against the armies of Russia, Prussia, and Spain. However, in 1812, Napoleon made the critical mistake of invading Russia. Together, fierce Russian resistance and the cruel Russian winter combined to break the back of the French Grand Armée. Of 450,000 Napoleonic troops in the Russian invasion, less than 20,000 survived the campaign. In 1815, at the Battle of Waterloo, Napoleon was finally defeated by the British led by the Duke of Wellington.

The British soldier pictured carries a flintlock musket fitted with a plug bayonet (inserted into the barrel). His musket was nicknamed the "Brown Bess." It fired a .75-caliber musket ball and was the standard British infantry weapon of this era. Although his uniform is colorful, it is less decorative and more utilitarian than those of the French troops.

CONFEDERATE INFANTRYMAN VS. UNION INFANTRYMAN (FACING PAGE), AMERICAN CIVIL WAR, 1861–1865

Confederate Infantryman

The American Civil War, sometimes called the "War Between the States," began in 1861 when eleven Southern states seceded from the United States. They formed their own independent nation known as the "Confederate States of America." They were opposed in this effort by the remaining twenty-three northern states, known as the "Union." The primary conflict between the North and South was centered on the problem of states' rights as it related to the issue of slavery.

The war was fought from 1861 to 1865 with a staggering loss of life on both sides. It is considered the first so-called "modern war" with massed barrages of advanced artillery, and huge armies of infantry and cavalry opposing one another along well-entrenched static battle lines. The Confederate forces won initial victories at the Battle of Bull Run (1861) and the Battle of

Fredericksburg (1862), led by the brilliant military tactician General Robert E. Lee.

The confederate soldier depicted carries an Enfield rifled musket supplied by the British. It fired a "Minie ball" out to an accurate distance of several hundred yards. Named after its inventor, French army captain Claude F. Minie, it was an improvement over the round ball used in smooth bore muskets. Its shape was conical—the classic "bullet-shape"—and featured an iron plug in the base. When fired, the impact of the gunpowder explosion forced the iron plug to drive the edges of the softer lead bullet into the spiral rifling inside the gun barrel. A flatter, more accurate bullet trajectory was the result. Confederate troops wore light gray uniforms that quickly faded to a butternut tan color when the dye oxidized on exposure to sunlight.

Union Infantryman

The Union forces during the Civil War had a decided advantage over the Confederates in terms of both manpower and industrial manufacturing capacity. While the initial momentum of the war favored the South, the ability of the North to sustain the war over a long period of time proved crucial. The Confederacy was facing critical shortages in both supplies and troops by 1863. The turning point of the war came in that same year at the Battle of Gettysburg when the South suffered a major defeat. By 1865, the Union army under General Ulysses S. Grant had captured Richmond, Virginia, the capital of the Confederacy. Finally, on April 9, 1865, General Lee surrendered to General Grant at Appomattox, Virginia, bringing the war to a close. The cost to both sides was enormous, with the number of battle casualties (killed and wounded) totalling over 600,000 American soldiers.

The Union trooper pictured carries a Springfield rifled musket similar to the Enfield used by the South. His uniform consists of a dark blue jacket and lighter blue trousers. The yellow chevrons on his sleeves denote his rank of sergeant.

FRENCH INFANTRYMAN VS. GERMAN INFANTRYMAN (FACING PAGE), WWI, 1914–1918

Entrenched French Infantryman

The First World War pitted the "Central Powers," Germany, Austria-Hungary, and Turkey, against the "Allied Powers," Great Britain, France, Russia, and later, the United States. From 1914 to 1918, huge armies faced each other across battlefield lines hundreds of miles long, producing the horror of "trench warfare," with soldiers dug into miles and miles of fortified earthen trenches. Opposing combatants tried continually to overrun and take the enemy positions, while batteries of thousands of cannon rained down destruction on each side's dug-in lines. The area between the two entrenched armies was called "No Man's Land," a blasted and cratered killing zone.

The French infantryman illustrated above waits in a well-fortified trench for the command to go "over the top" and attack across No Man's Land. The trench varies in depth from six to ten feet, and its dirt walls are reinforced with timber and sandbags. Many trenches were actually dug into the ground to form tunnels. These trench lines ran for miles and were protected at regular intervals by rapid-firing machine gun emplacements. The soldier's primary armament is a Lebel repeating rifle, a much improved weapon from the muzzle-loading rifles of the nineteenth century. It contained eight rounds of ammunition in a tubular storage chamber called a "magazine," located under the barrel. The rounds (bullets) were fed into the firing chamber by a semi-automatic bolt-action system so that soldiers could fire far more bullets in a much shorter time. This greatly improved "rate of fire" provided a distinct advantage on the battlefield.

German Infantryman Crossing No Man's Land

The battles of the First World War were often fought for mere yards of territory, gained with deadly attacks and counterattacks across the scarred area known as No Man's Land that separated the combatants' positions. When charging over this dangerous terrain, soldiers were exposed to individual rifle fire, machine guns spitting out hundreds of rounds per minute, artillery fire, and aerial bombardment. Thousands died in "stalemates"—deadlocked battles that could last for months or even years. Such huge losses could not be sustained by the Central Powers, especially with the addition of over 1 million fresh troops from the United States in 1918. Germany eventually surrendered to the Allies, signing the Treaty of Versailles in November 1918.

The German soldier depicted carries a Gewehr 98 repeating rifle with a fearsome eighteen-inch bayonet attached. The rifle held a five-round magazine that could be fired very quickly. His uniform is dark gray and his steel helmet is camouflaged with splotches of green, gray, and brown.

AFRIKA KORPS SOLDIER VS. BRITISH "DESERT RAT" (FACING PAGE), NORTH AFRICAN CAMPAIGN, WWII, 1939–1945

German Afrika Korps Soldier with Panzer III Battle Tank

From the ashes of Germany's defeat in the First World War rose the specter of an even more terrible global conflict—World War II. In a scant twenty-three years, German humiliation gave way to a fierce and destructive nationalism led by Adolf Hitler and his Nazi regime. In Europe, Hitler's 1939 invasion of Poland provoked World War II, with Britain and France allied against Germany. The military dictatorships of Germany, Italy, and Japan formed an alliance called the "Axis."

Axis partners Italy and Germany invaded Egypt in September 1940. Their goal was to gain control of the entire Mediterranean region as well as the crucial oil fields of the Middle East. By 1941, British armies were battling Axis forces throughout North Africa. The Germans fielded a specially trained and equipped

army to fight in the desert, the "Afrika Korps," led by the brilliant military tactician Field Marshall Erwin Rommel.

Shown above is a soldier of Rommel's Afrika Korps, armed with an MP40 submachine gun, widely used by Germany's mechanized infantry forces. A soldier could fire the thirty-two rounds contained in its magazine in a matter of seconds. The trooper also wears goggles to shield his eyes from the wind-blown dust and sand of the North African desert. In the background, a Panzer III battle tank rumbles forward. One of the early model German tanks of the war, the Panzer III was equipped with a 50-mm main cannon and two smaller machine guns. The word "Panzer" is short for *Panzer Kampfwagen* which means "armored battle vehicle."

British 8th Army "Desert Rat" with Churchill A22 Infantry Tank

Field Marshall Rommel was opposed in the North African campaign by the British 8th Army, nicknamed the "Desert Rats," under the command of Field Marshall Bernard Law Montgomery. In May 1942, the Germans achieved a major victory over the British at the Battle of Tobruk. But by the summer of 1942, the tide had turned against the Germans with the landing of an American army in North Africa to join the British. A decisive battle at El Alamein in October of 1942 resulted in a major German defeat. By 1943, the outnumbered and outgunned Afrika Korps was broken, caught between the allied British and American armies.

Depicted above is a British Desert Rat in a sandbagged defensive position. His weapon is the accurate and rugged Lee Enfield .303-caliber rifle, equipped with a ten-round magazine. It was the standard infantry weapon of the British forces and

remained in service until 1957. Parked beside him and waiting for action against advancing German Panzer forces is a "Churchill A22 Infantry Tank." A formidable and heavily armored vehicle, the Churchill mounted a 6-pounder 57-mm main cannon and two smaller machine guns.

In 1941, Hitler made the grievous error of invading the Soviet Union, thus committing his forces to a two-front war. Like Napoleon's army before him, the combination of Russian fighting tenacity and the brutal winter there decimated the invading Nazi army. Hundreds of thousands of German soldiers were killed or captured. The Allied invasion at Normandy in 1944 eventually led to the defeat of Hitler, caught between the Russians to the east and Americans and British to the west. A beaten and battered Germany surrendered in May 1945.

U.S. Marine Rifleman vs. Japanese Army Rifleman (facing page), Pacific Theater, WWII, 1941–1945

United States Marine Rifleman

The war in the Pacific began in December, 1941, with the Japanese attack on the American naval base at Pearl Harbor in the Hawaiian Islands. The United States responded by declaring war on Japan and its Axis partners, Germany and Italy.

By early 1942, Imperial Japan's army and navy had invaded and conquered all of southeast Asia including the Philippines and Indonesia. But major U.S. naval victories at the Battle of the Coral Sea and the Battle of Midway in mid-1942 halted Japanese expansion. These were the first great sea battles fought primarily between opposing aircraft carriers, changing the nature of navy surface warfare. The U.S. Navy and Marines

began a series of amphibious assaults on Pacific islands held by the Japanese. Capturing these islands was a key element in an eventual invasion of the Japanese mainland. Marine troops charged onto island beaches from specially designed landing ships and faced fierce resistance from dug-in Japanese soldiers. The heroism of the marines in the island battles of Tarawa, Guadalcanal, Iwo Jima, and Okinawa is legendary.

The American marine rifleman pictured wears a camouflage uniform and helmet of green, tan, and brown splotches designed to blend into the island's jungle environment. He carries the rugged and reliable M1 Garand semi-automatic rifle, a .30-caliber weapon with an eight-round magazine.

Japanese Imperial Army Rifleman

The Japanese troops such as the rifleman depicted above, were fanatically devoted to their emperor Hirohito. Fighting and dying for the emperor were considered sacred duties. This intense loyalty resulted in battles of incredible ferocity against American troops intent on dislodging the invaders from their captured territory. Casualties on both sides were enormous. However, by 1944 American forces had retaken many Japanese-held islands enabling them to establish U.S. airbases. These forward airfields allowed the new American long-range bomber, the B-29 "Superfortress," to strike at the Japanese homeland. Waves of U.S. bombers destroyed key military and industrial targets with deadly incendiary (fire) bombs. In August 1945, after the U.S. dropped the first atomic bombs on the cities of Hiroshima and Nagasaki, the war was effectively ended with Japan's unconditional surrender.